MW00927973

One Question a Day for You & Me

Five Year Journal Reflections for Couples

Copyright: **Published in the United States by Melissa Smith/ © 2019 Melissa Smith All right reserved.**

WWW.THEBOOKHIVE.NET
VISIT PAGE: FACEBOOK.COM/THEBOOKHIVEDOTNET

FOLLOW ME: AMAZON.COM/AUTHOR/MELISSAS

YOU

+

ME

=

AWESOME

January

1

What is your number one goal in life for this year?

YEAR _____

_____
_____
_____
_____

YEAR _____

_____
_____
_____
_____

YEAR _____

_____
_____
_____
_____

YEAR _____

_____
_____
_____
_____

YEAR _____

_____
_____
_____
_____

January

2

Who was the last person to tell you "I love you" ?

YEAR _____
_____
_____
_____
_____

YEAR _____
_____
_____
_____
_____

YEAR _____
_____
_____
_____
_____

YEAR _____
_____
_____
_____
_____

YEAR _____
_____
_____
_____
_____

January

3

What was one of the hardest things
You have dealt with last year?

YEAR_____
_____
_____
_____
_____

YEAR_____
_____
_____
_____
_____

YEAR_____
_____
_____
_____
_____

YEAR_____
_____
_____
_____
_____

YEAR_____
_____
_____
_____
_____

January

4

What's the best part of your day?

YEAR _____

_____
_____
_____
_____

YEAR _____

_____
_____
_____
_____

YEAR _____

_____
_____
_____
_____

YEAR _____

_____
_____
_____
_____

YEAR _____

_____
_____
_____
_____

January

5

What made your day unusual?

YEAR _____

_____
_____
_____
_____

YEAR _____

_____
_____
_____
_____

YEAR _____

_____
_____
_____
_____

YEAR _____

_____
_____
_____
_____

YEAR _____

_____
_____
_____
_____

January

6

What have you done today?

YEAR _____
_____
_____
_____
_____

YEAR _____
_____
_____
_____
_____

YEAR _____
_____
_____
_____
_____

YEAR _____
_____
_____
_____
_____

YEAR _____
_____
_____
_____
_____

January

7

What was your last major purchase?

YEAR _____

_____
_____
_____
_____

YEAR _____

_____
_____
_____
_____

YEAR _____

_____
_____
_____
_____

YEAR _____

_____
_____
_____
_____

YEAR _____

_____
_____
_____
_____

January

8

What are you looking for in your life?

YEAR _____

_____
_____
_____
_____

YEAR _____

_____
_____
_____
_____

YEAR _____

_____
_____
_____
_____

YEAR _____

_____
_____
_____
_____

YEAR _____

_____
_____
_____
_____

January

9

Cake or cookie?

YEAR _____

_____
_____
_____
_____

YEAR _____

_____
_____
_____
_____

YEAR _____

_____
_____
_____
_____

YEAR _____

_____
_____
_____
_____

YEAR _____

_____
_____
_____
_____

January

10

How can you make the world a better place?

YEAR _____

_____
_____
_____
_____

YEAR _____

_____
_____
_____
_____

YEAR _____

_____
_____
_____
_____

YEAR _____

_____
_____
_____
_____

YEAR _____

_____
_____
_____
_____

January

11

What is your first childhood memory?

YEAR _____

_____
_____
_____
_____

YEAR _____

_____
_____
_____
_____

YEAR _____

_____
_____
_____
_____

YEAR _____

_____
_____
_____
_____

YEAR _____

_____
_____
_____
_____

January

12

Who do you admire the most and why?

YEAR_____

_____
_____
_____
_____

YEAR_____

_____
_____
_____
_____

YEAR_____

_____
_____
_____
_____

YEAR_____

_____
_____
_____
_____

YEAR_____

_____
_____
_____
_____

January

13

Are you a morning or a night person?

YEAR _____

_____

_____

_____

_____

YEAR _____

_____

_____

_____

_____

YEAR _____

_____

_____

_____

_____

YEAR _____

_____

_____

_____

_____

YEAR _____

_____

_____

_____

_____

January

14

Three things you cannot live without.

YEAR _____
_____
_____
_____
_____

YEAR _____
_____
_____
_____
_____

YEAR _____
_____
_____
_____
_____

YEAR _____
_____
_____
_____
_____

YEAR _____
_____
_____
_____
_____

January

15

Which event in your life
had the biggest impact on your life
and your personality?

YEAR _____

_____
_____
_____
_____

YEAR _____

_____
_____
_____
_____

YEAR _____

_____
_____
_____
_____

YEAR _____

_____
_____
_____
_____

YEAR _____

_____
_____
_____
_____

January

16

What would you do if you had only 24 hours to live?

YEAR_____

_____
_____
_____
_____

YEAR_____

_____
_____
_____
_____

YEAR_____

_____
_____
_____
_____

YEAR_____

_____
_____
_____
_____

YEAR_____

_____
_____
_____
_____

January

17

What activities do you absolutely love doing?

YEAR _____

_____
_____
_____
_____

YEAR _____

_____
_____
_____
_____

YEAR _____

_____
_____
_____
_____

YEAR _____

_____
_____
_____
_____

YEAR _____

_____
_____
_____
_____

January

18

Five things you are most grateful for
in your life right now.

YEAR _____

_____

_____

_____

_____

YEAR _____

_____

_____

_____

_____

YEAR _____

_____

_____

_____

_____

YEAR _____

_____

_____

_____

_____

YEAR _____

_____

_____

_____

_____

January

19

If you would live anywhere in the world,
where would it be?

YEAR _____

_____
_____
_____
_____

YEAR _____

_____
_____
_____
_____

YEAR _____

_____
_____
_____
_____

YEAR _____

_____
_____
_____
_____

YEAR _____

_____
_____
_____
_____

January

Your 3 favorite songs right now.

YEAR _____

_____
_____
_____
_____

YEAR _____

_____
_____
_____
_____

YEAR _____

_____
_____
_____
_____

YEAR _____

_____
_____
_____
_____

YEAR _____

_____
_____
_____
_____

January

21

If you could donate $1,000,000 to any charity, which would you choose and why?

YEAR _____

_____

_____

_____

_____

YEAR _____

_____

_____

_____

_____

YEAR _____

_____

_____

_____

_____

YEAR _____

_____

_____

_____

_____

YEAR _____

_____

_____

_____

_____

January

22

What is the best gift you have ever received?

YEAR _____

_____
_____
_____
_____

YEAR _____

_____
_____
_____
_____

YEAR _____

_____
_____
_____
_____

YEAR _____

_____
_____
_____
_____

YEAR _____

_____
_____
_____
_____

January

23

What do you wish you would be remembered for in your life?

YEAR _____

_____
_____
_____
_____

YEAR _____

_____
_____
_____
_____

YEAR _____

_____
_____
_____
_____

YEAR _____

_____
_____
_____
_____

YEAR _____

_____
_____
_____
_____

January

24

What is the meaning behind your smile today?

YEAR_____

_____
_____
_____
_____

YEAR_____

_____
_____
_____
_____

YEAR_____

_____
_____
_____
_____

YEAR_____

_____
_____
_____
_____

YEAR_____

_____
_____
_____
_____

January

25

Who was the last person you hugged?

YEAR _____

_____
_____
_____
_____

YEAR _____

_____
_____
_____
_____

YEAR _____

_____
_____
_____
_____

YEAR _____

_____
_____
_____
_____

YEAR _____

_____
_____
_____
_____

January

26

What is your biggest addiction?

YEAR _____

_____
_____
_____
_____

YEAR _____

_____
_____
_____
_____

YEAR _____

_____
_____
_____
_____

YEAR _____

_____
_____
_____
_____

YEAR _____

_____
_____
_____
_____

January

27

What are 3 things you regret doing in your life?

YEAR _____

_____

_____

_____

_____

YEAR _____

_____

_____

_____

_____

YEAR _____

_____

_____

_____

_____

YEAR _____

_____

_____

_____

_____

YEAR _____

_____

_____

_____

_____

January

28

What are your short-term goals for this month?
(Give at least 5)

YEAR _____

_____
_____
_____
_____

YEAR _____

_____
_____
_____
_____

YEAR _____

_____
_____
_____
_____

YEAR _____

_____
_____
_____
_____

YEAR _____

_____
_____
_____
_____

January

29

Who is your favorite superhero and why?

YEAR _____

_____
_____
_____
_____

YEAR _____

_____
_____
_____
_____

YEAR _____

_____
_____
_____
_____

YEAR _____

_____
_____
_____
_____

YEAR _____

_____
_____
_____
_____

January

30

What is your dream job?

YEAR_____

_____
_____
_____
_____

YEAR_____

_____
_____
_____
_____

YEAR_____

_____
_____
_____
_____

YEAR_____

_____
_____
_____
_____

YEAR_____

_____
_____
_____
_____

January

31

Ability to fly or Invisibility?

YEAR _____

_____
_____
_____
_____

YEAR _____

_____
_____
_____
_____

YEAR _____

_____
_____
_____
_____

YEAR _____

_____
_____
_____
_____

YEAR _____

_____
_____
_____
_____

February

1

What would you do with your "15 minutes of fame"?

YEAR _____

_____
_____
_____
_____

YEAR _____

_____
_____
_____
_____

YEAR _____

_____
_____
_____
_____

YEAR _____

_____
_____
_____
_____

YEAR _____

_____
_____
_____
_____

February

2

What is your favorite TV show right now?

YEAR _____

_____
_____
_____
_____

YEAR _____

_____
_____
_____
_____

YEAR _____

_____
_____
_____
_____

YEAR _____

_____
_____
_____
_____

YEAR _____

_____
_____
_____
_____

February

3

What is your opinion on second chances?

YEAR _____

_____

_____

_____

_____

YEAR _____

_____

_____

_____

_____

YEAR _____

_____

_____

_____

_____

YEAR _____

_____

_____

_____

_____

YEAR _____

_____

_____

_____

_____

February

4

Have you ever gotten any tattoo? What is it?

YEAR_____

_____
_____
_____
_____

YEAR_____

_____
_____
_____
_____

YEAR_____

_____
_____
_____
_____

YEAR_____

_____
_____
_____
_____

YEAR_____

_____
_____
_____
_____

February

5

Do you believe in love at first sight?

YEAR _____

_____
_____
_____
_____

YEAR _____

_____
_____
_____
_____

YEAR _____

_____
_____
_____
_____

YEAR _____

_____
_____
_____
_____

YEAR _____

_____
_____
_____
_____

February

6

Are you a jealous person? How jealous?

YEAR _____

_____
_____
_____
_____

YEAR _____

_____
_____
_____
_____

YEAR _____

_____
_____
_____
_____

YEAR _____

_____
_____
_____
_____

YEAR _____

_____
_____
_____
_____

February

7

Who was the last person you talked to?

YEAR_____

_____
_____
_____
_____

YEAR_____

_____
_____
_____
_____

YEAR_____

_____
_____
_____
_____

YEAR_____

_____
_____
_____
_____

YEAR_____

_____
_____
_____
_____

February

8

What is your longest relationship?

YEAR _____

_____
_____
_____
_____

YEAR _____

_____
_____
_____
_____

YEAR _____

_____
_____
_____
_____

YEAR _____

_____
_____
_____
_____

YEAR _____

_____
_____
_____
_____

February

9

Are you a heavy sleeper?

YEAR _____

_____
_____
_____
_____

YEAR _____

_____
_____
_____
_____

YEAR _____

_____
_____
_____
_____

YEAR _____

_____
_____
_____
_____

YEAR _____

_____
_____
_____
_____

February

10

What should you be doing right now?

YEAR _____
_____
_____
_____
_____

YEAR _____
_____
_____
_____
_____

YEAR _____
_____
_____
_____
_____

YEAR _____
_____
_____
_____
_____

YEAR _____
_____
_____
_____
_____

February

11

Who is your best friend?

YEAR _____

_____
_____
_____
_____

YEAR _____

_____
_____
_____
_____

YEAR _____

_____
_____
_____
_____

YEAR _____

_____
_____
_____
_____

YEAR _____

_____
_____
_____
_____

February

12

What is your favorite book right now?

YEAR _____

_____
_____
_____
_____

YEAR _____

_____
_____
_____
_____

YEAR _____

_____
_____
_____
_____

YEAR _____

_____
_____
_____
_____

YEAR _____

_____
_____
_____
_____

February

13

Do you cry easily?

YEAR _____

_____
_____
_____
_____

YEAR _____

_____
_____
_____
_____

YEAR _____

_____
_____
_____
_____

YEAR _____

_____
_____
_____
_____

YEAR _____

_____
_____
_____
_____

February

14

If your life was a novel, what would be the title?

YEAR _____

_____
_____
_____
_____

YEAR _____

_____
_____
_____
_____

YEAR _____

_____
_____
_____
_____

YEAR _____

_____
_____
_____
_____

YEAR _____

_____
_____
_____
_____

February

15

Does anyone like you?

YEAR _____

_____
_____
_____
_____

YEAR _____

_____
_____
_____
_____

YEAR _____

_____
_____
_____
_____

YEAR _____

_____
_____
_____
_____

YEAR _____

_____
_____
_____
_____

February

16

If you could spend one day in someone else's shoes,
who would it be and why?

YEAR _____

_____
_____
_____
_____

YEAR _____

_____
_____
_____
_____

YEAR _____

_____
_____
_____
_____

YEAR _____

_____
_____
_____
_____

YEAR _____

_____
_____
_____
_____

February

17

Have you ever broken up with someone?

YEAR _____

_____
_____
_____
_____

YEAR _____

_____
_____
_____
_____

YEAR _____

_____
_____
_____
_____

YEAR _____

_____
_____
_____
_____

YEAR _____

_____
_____
_____
_____

February

18

Who do you feel most comfortable talking to about anything?

YEAR _____

_____

_____

_____

_____

YEAR _____

_____

_____

_____

_____

YEAR _____

_____

_____

_____

_____

YEAR _____

_____

_____

_____

_____

YEAR _____

_____

_____

_____

_____

February

19

Do you have any phobias?

YEAR _____

YEAR _____

YEAR _____

YEAR _____

YEAR _____

February

20

Which do you prefer, scuba diving or hiking?

YEAR _____
_____
_____
_____
_____

YEAR _____
_____
_____
_____
_____

YEAR _____
_____
_____
_____
_____

YEAR _____
_____
_____
_____
_____

YEAR _____
_____
_____
_____
_____

February

21

Do you fall for people easily?

YEAR_____

_____
_____
_____
_____

YEAR_____

_____
_____
_____
_____

YEAR_____

_____
_____
_____
_____

YEAR_____

_____
_____
_____
_____

YEAR_____

_____
_____
_____
_____

February

22

What is your favorite candy?

YEAR _____

_____
_____
_____
_____

YEAR _____

_____
_____
_____
_____

YEAR _____

_____
_____
_____
_____

YEAR _____

_____
_____
_____
_____

YEAR _____

_____
_____
_____
_____

February

23

If you were going to bury a time capsule,
what would you put in it?

YEAR _____

_____
_____
_____
_____

YEAR _____

_____
_____
_____
_____

YEAR _____

_____
_____
_____
_____

YEAR _____

_____
_____
_____
_____

YEAR _____

_____
_____
_____
_____

February

What are five ways to win your heart?

YEAR _____
_____
_____
_____
_____

YEAR _____
_____
_____
_____
_____

YEAR _____
_____
_____
_____
_____

YEAR _____
_____
_____
_____
_____

YEAR _____
_____
_____
_____
_____

February

25

Do you get butterflies around the person you like?

YEAR _____

_____
_____
_____
_____

YEAR _____

_____
_____
_____
_____

YEAR _____

_____
_____
_____
_____

YEAR _____

_____
_____
_____
_____

YEAR _____

_____
_____
_____
_____

February

26

What are your thoughts about long distance relationships?

YEAR _____

_____
_____
_____
_____

YEAR _____

_____
_____
_____
_____

YEAR _____

_____
_____
_____
_____

YEAR _____

_____
_____
_____
_____

YEAR _____

_____
_____
_____
_____

February

27

What is your opinion about your body?

YEAR _____

_____
_____
_____
_____

YEAR _____

_____
_____
_____
_____

YEAR _____

_____
_____
_____
_____

YEAR _____

_____
_____
_____
_____

YEAR _____

_____
_____
_____
_____

February

28

What is your favorite childhood memory?

YEAR _____

_____
_____
_____
_____

YEAR _____

_____
_____
_____
_____

YEAR _____

_____
_____
_____
_____

YEAR _____

_____
_____
_____
_____

YEAR _____

_____
_____
_____
_____

February

29

How important do you think education is?

YEAR _____

_____

_____

_____

_____

YEAR _____

_____

_____

_____

_____

YEAR _____

_____

_____

_____

_____

YEAR _____

_____

_____

_____

_____

YEAR _____

_____

_____

_____

_____

March

1

What is one thing you wish you own?

YEAR _____

_____
_____
_____
_____

YEAR _____

_____
_____
_____
_____

YEAR _____

_____
_____
_____
_____

YEAR _____

_____
_____
_____
_____

YEAR _____

_____
_____
_____
_____

March

2

What annoys you the most?

YEAR _____
_____
_____
_____
_____

YEAR _____
_____
_____
_____
_____

YEAR _____
_____
_____
_____
_____

YEAR _____
_____
_____
_____
_____

YEAR _____
_____
_____
_____
_____

March

3

How do you feel about animals and pets?

YEAR _____

_____
_____
_____
_____

YEAR _____

_____
_____
_____
_____

YEAR _____

_____
_____
_____
_____

YEAR _____

_____
_____
_____
_____

YEAR _____

_____
_____
_____
_____

March

4

What did you learn too late in life?

YEAR _____

_____
_____
_____
_____

YEAR _____

_____
_____
_____
_____

YEAR _____

_____
_____
_____
_____

YEAR _____

_____
_____
_____
_____

YEAR _____

_____
_____
_____
_____

March

5

Who is your favorite author?

YEAR _____

_____
_____
_____
_____

YEAR _____

_____
_____
_____
_____

YEAR _____

_____
_____
_____
_____

YEAR _____

_____
_____
_____
_____

YEAR _____

_____
_____
_____
_____

March

6

Coke or Pepsi?

YEAR_____

YEAR_____

YEAR_____

YEAR_____

YEAR_____

March

7

What three simple things are you most thankful for in your life today?

YEAR _____

_____

_____

_____

_____

YEAR _____

_____

_____

_____

_____

YEAR _____

_____

_____

_____

_____

YEAR _____

_____

_____

_____

_____

YEAR _____

_____

_____

_____

_____

March

8

Who is on your mind at this moment?

YEAR _____

_____
_____
_____
_____

YEAR _____

_____
_____
_____
_____

YEAR _____

_____
_____
_____
_____

YEAR _____

_____
_____
_____
_____

YEAR _____

_____
_____
_____
_____

March

9

Are you forgiving?

YEAR _____

_____
_____
_____
_____

YEAR _____

_____
_____
_____
_____

YEAR _____

_____
_____
_____
_____

YEAR _____

_____
_____
_____
_____

YEAR _____

_____
_____
_____
_____

March

10

What is your favorite accessory?

YEAR _____

_____
_____
_____
_____

YEAR _____

_____
_____
_____
_____

YEAR _____

_____
_____
_____
_____

YEAR _____

_____
_____
_____
_____

YEAR _____

_____
_____
_____
_____

March

11

What was the temperature today?

YEAR _____

_____
_____
_____
_____

YEAR _____

_____
_____
_____
_____

YEAR _____

_____
_____
_____
_____

YEAR _____

_____
_____
_____
_____

YEAR _____

_____
_____
_____
_____

March

12

What are you passionate about?

YEAR _____

_____
_____
_____
_____

YEAR _____

_____
_____
_____
_____

YEAR _____

_____
_____
_____
_____

YEAR _____

_____
_____
_____
_____

YEAR _____

_____
_____
_____
_____

March

13

What are your favorite websites?

YEAR _____

_____
_____
_____
_____

YEAR _____

_____
_____
_____
_____

YEAR _____

_____
_____
_____
_____

YEAR _____

_____
_____
_____
_____

YEAR _____

_____
_____
_____
_____

March
14

How is your relationship with your parents?

YEAR _____

_____
_____
_____
_____

YEAR _____

_____
_____
_____
_____

YEAR _____

_____
_____
_____
_____

YEAR _____

_____
_____
_____
_____

YEAR _____

_____
_____
_____
_____

March

15

Any traumatic experience lately?

YEAR _____

_____

_____

_____

_____

YEAR _____

_____

_____

_____

_____

YEAR _____

_____

_____

_____

_____

YEAR _____

_____

_____

_____

_____

YEAR _____

_____

_____

_____

_____

March

16

Your biggest turn on.

YEAR _____

_____
_____
_____
_____

YEAR _____

_____
_____
_____
_____

YEAR _____

_____
_____
_____
_____

YEAR _____

_____
_____
_____
_____

YEAR _____

_____
_____
_____
_____

March
17

What are your hopes for your children?

YEAR _____
_____
_____
_____
_____

YEAR _____
_____
_____
_____
_____

YEAR _____
_____
_____
_____
_____

YEAR _____
_____
_____
_____
_____

YEAR _____
_____
_____
_____
_____

March

18

What is your Monday morning routine?

YEAR _____

_____

_____

_____

_____

YEAR _____

_____

_____

_____

_____

YEAR _____

_____

_____

_____

_____

YEAR _____

_____

_____

_____

_____

YEAR _____

_____

_____

_____

_____

March

19

How would you spend an entire day alone?

YEAR _____

_____
_____
_____
_____

YEAR _____

_____
_____
_____
_____

YEAR _____

_____
_____
_____
_____

YEAR _____

_____
_____
_____
_____

YEAR _____

_____
_____
_____
_____

March

20

What was the best part about growing up?

YEAR _____

_____

_____

_____

_____

YEAR _____

_____

_____

_____

_____

YEAR _____

_____

_____

_____

_____

YEAR _____

_____

_____

_____

_____

YEAR _____

_____

_____

_____

_____

March

21

Your recent white lie and why.

YEAR _____

_____
_____
_____
_____

YEAR _____

_____
_____
_____
_____

YEAR _____

_____
_____
_____
_____

YEAR _____

_____
_____
_____
_____

YEAR _____

_____
_____
_____
_____

March

22

What is your comfort food now?

YEAR _____

_____

_____

_____

_____

YEAR _____

_____

_____

_____

_____

YEAR _____

_____

_____

_____

_____

YEAR _____

_____

_____

_____

_____

YEAR _____

_____

_____

_____

_____

March

23

Something that motivated you this month.

YEAR _____

_____
_____
_____
_____

YEAR _____

_____
_____
_____
_____

YEAR _____

_____
_____
_____
_____

YEAR _____

_____
_____
_____
_____

YEAR _____

_____
_____
_____
_____

March

How are you feeling today?

YEAR _____

_____
_____
_____
_____

YEAR _____

_____
_____
_____
_____

YEAR _____

_____
_____
_____
_____

YEAR _____

_____
_____
_____
_____

YEAR _____

_____
_____
_____
_____

March

25

What's a Quote you try to live by?

YEAR _____

_____

_____

_____

_____

YEAR _____

_____

_____

_____

_____

YEAR _____

_____

_____

_____

_____

YEAR _____

_____

_____

_____

_____

YEAR _____

_____

_____

_____

_____

March

26

What is something you are proud of?

YEAR _____

_____
_____
_____
_____

YEAR _____

_____
_____
_____
_____

YEAR _____

_____
_____
_____
_____

YEAR _____

_____
_____
_____
_____

YEAR _____

_____
_____
_____
_____

March

27

A recent blessing in disguise.

YEAR _____
_____
_____
_____
_____

YEAR _____
_____
_____
_____
_____

YEAR _____
_____
_____
_____
_____

YEAR _____
_____
_____
_____
_____

YEAR _____
_____
_____
_____
_____

March

28

3 tangible goals for the month ahead.

YEAR _____

_____
_____
_____
_____

YEAR _____

_____
_____
_____
_____

YEAR _____

_____
_____
_____
_____

YEAR _____

_____
_____
_____
_____

YEAR _____

_____
_____
_____
_____

March

29

What was the last gift you gave
that made someone very happy?

YEAR _____

_____
_____
_____
_____

YEAR _____

_____
_____
_____
_____

YEAR _____

_____
_____
_____
_____

YEAR _____

_____
_____
_____
_____

YEAR _____

_____
_____
_____
_____

March

30

Are you in debt now? Why?

YEAR _____

_____
_____
_____
_____

YEAR _____

_____
_____
_____
_____

YEAR _____

_____
_____
_____
_____

YEAR _____

_____
_____
_____
_____

YEAR _____

_____
_____
_____
_____

March

31

How did you improve yourself in the past few months?

YEAR _____

_____
_____
_____
_____

YEAR _____

_____
_____
_____
_____

YEAR _____

_____
_____
_____
_____

YEAR _____

_____
_____
_____
_____

YEAR _____

_____
_____
_____
_____

April

1

Has anyone pulled a prank on you today?
What did they do?

YEAR _____

_____
_____
_____
_____

YEAR _____

_____
_____
_____
_____

YEAR _____

_____
_____
_____
_____

YEAR _____

_____
_____
_____
_____

YEAR _____

_____
_____
_____
_____

April

2

If you could be an animal, what would it be and why?

YEAR _____

_____
_____
_____
_____

YEAR _____

_____
_____
_____
_____

YEAR _____

_____
_____
_____
_____

YEAR _____

_____
_____
_____
_____

YEAR _____

_____
_____
_____
_____

April

3

What made you nervous lately?

YEAR _____

_____

_____

_____

_____

YEAR _____

_____

_____

_____

_____

YEAR _____

_____

_____

_____

_____

YEAR _____

_____

_____

_____

_____

YEAR _____

_____

_____

_____

_____

April

4

Describe you ideal vacation.

YEAR_____

_____
_____
_____
_____

YEAR_____

_____
_____
_____
_____

YEAR_____

_____
_____
_____
_____

YEAR_____

_____
_____
_____
_____

YEAR_____

_____
_____
_____
_____

April

5

What are you struggling with right now?

YEAR _____

_____
_____
_____
_____

YEAR _____

_____
_____
_____
_____

YEAR _____

_____
_____
_____
_____

YEAR _____

_____
_____
_____
_____

YEAR _____

_____
_____
_____
_____

April

6

Have you ever been awake for 32 hours straight?

YEAR_____

_____
_____
_____
_____

YEAR_____

_____
_____
_____
_____

YEAR_____

_____
_____
_____
_____

YEAR_____

_____
_____
_____
_____

YEAR_____

_____
_____
_____
_____

April

7

Who was the last person you drive with?

YEAR_____

_____
_____
_____
_____

YEAR_____

_____
_____
_____
_____

YEAR_____

_____
_____
_____
_____

YEAR_____

_____
_____
_____
_____

YEAR_____

_____
_____
_____
_____

April

8

What do you hate most about work?

YEAR _____

_____

_____

_____

_____

YEAR _____

_____

_____

_____

_____

YEAR _____

_____

_____

_____

_____

YEAR _____

_____

_____

_____

_____

YEAR _____

_____

_____

_____

_____

April

9

What do you find attractive in a person?

YEAR _____

_____

_____

_____

_____

YEAR _____

_____

_____

_____

_____

YEAR _____

_____

_____

_____

_____

YEAR _____

_____

_____

_____

_____

YEAR _____

_____

_____

_____

_____

April

10

How many true friends do you have now?

YEAR _____

_____
_____
_____
_____

YEAR _____

_____
_____
_____
_____

YEAR _____

_____
_____
_____
_____

YEAR _____

_____
_____
_____
_____

YEAR _____

_____
_____
_____
_____

April

11

How is your relationship with your siblings?

YEAR _____

_____
_____
_____
_____

YEAR _____

_____
_____
_____
_____

YEAR _____

_____
_____
_____
_____

YEAR _____

_____
_____
_____
_____

YEAR _____

_____
_____
_____
_____

April

12

What does it mean to be courageous?

YEAR _____

_____

_____

_____

_____

YEAR _____

_____

_____

_____

_____

YEAR _____

_____

_____

_____

_____

YEAR _____

_____

_____

_____

_____

YEAR _____

_____

_____

_____

_____

April

13

What's your favorite outfit?

YEAR_____

_____
_____
_____
_____

YEAR_____

_____
_____
_____
_____

YEAR_____

_____
_____
_____
_____

YEAR_____

_____
_____
_____
_____

YEAR_____

_____
_____
_____
_____

April

14

List 5 weird things that you like.

YEAR _____

_____

_____

_____

_____

YEAR _____

_____

_____

_____

_____

YEAR _____

_____

_____

_____

_____

YEAR _____

_____

_____

_____

_____

YEAR _____

_____

_____

_____

_____

April

15

If you could spend a day in someone else's shoes,
who would it be and why?

YEAR _____

_____
_____
_____
_____

YEAR _____

_____
_____
_____
_____

YEAR _____

_____
_____
_____
_____

YEAR _____

_____
_____
_____
_____

YEAR _____

_____
_____
_____
_____

April

16

What are the achievements you are most proud of?

YEAR_____
_____
_____
_____
_____

YEAR_____
_____
_____
_____
_____

YEAR_____
_____
_____
_____
_____

YEAR_____
_____
_____
_____
_____

YEAR_____
_____
_____
_____
_____

April

17

Burger or Pizza?

YEAR _____

_____

_____

_____

_____

YEAR _____

_____

_____

_____

_____

YEAR _____

_____

_____

_____

_____

YEAR _____

_____

_____

_____

_____

YEAR _____

_____

_____

_____

_____

April

18

Your favorite genre in music.

YEAR_____

_____
_____
_____
_____

YEAR_____

_____
_____
_____
_____

YEAR_____

_____
_____
_____
_____

YEAR_____

_____
_____
_____
_____

YEAR_____

_____
_____
_____
_____

April

19

What's the last thing you purchased?

YEAR _____

_____

_____

_____

_____

YEAR _____

_____

_____

_____

_____

YEAR _____

_____

_____

_____

_____

YEAR _____

_____

_____

_____

_____

YEAR _____

_____

_____

_____

_____

April

20

What would you like more of in your life right now?

YEAR _____

_____
_____
_____
_____

YEAR _____

_____
_____
_____
_____

YEAR _____

_____
_____
_____
_____

YEAR _____

_____
_____
_____
_____

YEAR _____

_____
_____
_____
_____

April

21

Do you believe in soul mates?

YEAR _____

_____
_____
_____
_____

YEAR _____

_____
_____
_____
_____

YEAR _____

_____
_____
_____
_____

YEAR _____

_____
_____
_____
_____

YEAR _____

_____
_____
_____
_____

April

22

What's your favorite memory of today?

YEAR _____

_____

_____

_____

_____

YEAR _____

_____

_____

_____

_____

YEAR _____

_____

_____

_____

_____

YEAR _____

_____

_____

_____

_____

YEAR _____

_____

_____

_____

_____

April

23

Who do you envy?

YEAR _____

_____

_____

_____

_____

YEAR _____

_____

_____

_____

_____

YEAR _____

_____

_____

_____

_____

YEAR _____

_____

_____

_____

_____

YEAR _____

_____

_____

_____

_____

April

24

Describe your idea of a perfect date.

YEAR _____

_____

_____

_____

_____

YEAR _____

_____

_____

_____

_____

YEAR _____

_____

_____

_____

_____

YEAR _____

_____

_____

_____

_____

YEAR _____

_____

_____

_____

_____

April

25

What do you want to see more of in your life?

YEAR _____

_____
_____
_____
_____

YEAR _____

_____
_____
_____
_____

YEAR _____

_____
_____
_____
_____

YEAR _____

_____
_____
_____
_____

YEAR _____

_____
_____
_____
_____

April

26

Three things you can't live without.

YEAR _____

_____
_____
_____
_____

YEAR _____

_____
_____
_____
_____

YEAR _____

_____
_____
_____
_____

YEAR _____

_____
_____
_____
_____

YEAR _____

_____
_____
_____
_____

April

27

What bad habits do you want to break?

YEAR _____

_____
_____
_____
_____

YEAR _____

_____
_____
_____
_____

YEAR _____

_____
_____
_____
_____

YEAR _____

_____
_____
_____
_____

YEAR _____

_____
_____
_____
_____

April

28

Describe your last dance.

YEAR _____

_____
_____
_____
_____

YEAR _____

_____
_____
_____
_____

YEAR _____

_____
_____
_____
_____

YEAR _____

_____
_____
_____
_____

YEAR _____

_____
_____
_____
_____

April

29

When was the last time you did something risky?

YEAR _____

_____
_____
_____
_____

YEAR _____

_____
_____
_____
_____

YEAR _____

_____
_____
_____
_____

YEAR _____

_____
_____
_____
_____

YEAR _____

_____
_____
_____
_____

April

30

What do you love most about yourself?

YEAR _____

_____
_____
_____
_____

YEAR _____

_____
_____
_____
_____

YEAR _____

_____
_____
_____
_____

YEAR _____

_____
_____
_____
_____

YEAR _____

_____
_____
_____
_____

May

1

What is a funny thing that happened today?

YEAR_____

_____
_____
_____
_____

YEAR_____

_____
_____
_____
_____

YEAR_____

_____
_____
_____
_____

YEAR_____

_____
_____
_____
_____

YEAR_____

_____
_____
_____
_____

May

2

What was your horoscope today?

YEAR _____

_____
_____
_____
_____

YEAR _____

_____
_____
_____
_____

YEAR _____

_____
_____
_____
_____

YEAR _____

_____
_____
_____
_____

YEAR _____

_____
_____
_____
_____

May

3

The best compliment you received lately.

YEAR _____

_____
_____
_____
_____

YEAR _____

_____
_____
_____
_____

YEAR _____

_____
_____
_____
_____

YEAR _____

_____
_____
_____
_____

YEAR _____

_____
_____
_____
_____

May

4

If you could go back in time,
what would you say to your younger self?

YEAR_____

_____
_____
_____
_____

YEAR_____

_____
_____
_____
_____

YEAR_____

_____
_____
_____
_____

YEAR_____

_____
_____
_____
_____

YEAR_____

_____
_____
_____
_____

May

5

What is your philosophy in life?

YEAR _____

_____
_____
_____
_____

YEAR _____

_____
_____
_____
_____

YEAR _____

_____
_____
_____
_____

YEAR _____

_____
_____
_____
_____

YEAR _____

_____
_____
_____
_____

May

6

A recent mistake that impacted your life positively.

YEAR _____

_____
_____
_____
_____

YEAR _____

_____
_____
_____
_____

YEAR _____

_____
_____
_____
_____

YEAR _____

_____
_____
_____
_____

YEAR _____

_____
_____
_____
_____

May
7

Name 5 good things you want to do better at.

YEAR _____

_____
_____
_____
_____

YEAR _____

_____
_____
_____
_____

YEAR _____

_____
_____
_____
_____

YEAR _____

_____
_____
_____
_____

YEAR _____

_____
_____
_____
_____

May

8

Is fame important?

YEAR _____

_____
_____
_____
_____

YEAR _____

_____
_____
_____
_____

YEAR _____

_____
_____
_____
_____

YEAR _____

_____
_____
_____
_____

YEAR _____

_____
_____
_____
_____

May

9

Are you organized or messy?

YEAR_____

_____
_____
_____
_____

YEAR_____

_____
_____
_____
_____

YEAR_____

_____
_____
_____
_____

YEAR_____

_____
_____
_____
_____

YEAR_____

_____
_____
_____
_____

May

10

How is the weather outside?

YEAR _____

_____
_____
_____
_____

YEAR _____

_____
_____
_____
_____

YEAR _____

_____
_____
_____
_____

YEAR _____

_____
_____
_____
_____

YEAR _____

_____
_____
_____
_____

May

11

Describe your dream house.

YEAR _____

_____
_____
_____
_____

YEAR _____

_____
_____
_____
_____

YEAR _____

_____
_____
_____
_____

YEAR _____

_____
_____
_____
_____

YEAR _____

_____
_____
_____
_____

May

12

Fruits or Vegetables?

YEAR _____

_____
_____
_____
_____

YEAR _____

_____
_____
_____
_____

YEAR _____

_____
_____
_____
_____

YEAR _____

_____
_____
_____
_____

YEAR _____

_____
_____
_____
_____

May

13

When was the last time you had a good laugh?

YEAR _____

_____
_____
_____
_____

YEAR _____

_____
_____
_____
_____

YEAR _____

_____
_____
_____
_____

YEAR _____

_____
_____
_____
_____

YEAR _____

_____
_____
_____
_____

May
14

What is the meaning of life?

YEAR _____

_____
_____
_____
_____

YEAR _____

_____
_____
_____
_____

YEAR _____

_____
_____
_____
_____

YEAR _____

_____
_____
_____
_____

YEAR _____

_____
_____
_____
_____

May

15

What is your guilty pleasure?

YEAR _____

_____
_____
_____
_____

YEAR _____

_____
_____
_____
_____

YEAR _____

_____
_____
_____
_____

YEAR _____

_____
_____
_____
_____

YEAR _____

_____
_____
_____
_____

May

16

What is your hairstyle?

YEAR _____

_____
_____
_____
_____

YEAR _____

_____
_____
_____
_____

YEAR _____

_____
_____
_____
_____

YEAR _____

_____
_____
_____
_____

YEAR _____

_____
_____
_____
_____

May
17

What was the best breakfast you had recently?

YEAR_____

_____
_____
_____
_____

YEAR_____

_____
_____
_____
_____

YEAR_____

_____
_____
_____
_____

YEAR_____

_____
_____
_____
_____

YEAR_____

_____
_____
_____
_____

May

18

Who is your celebrity crush now?

YEAR _____

_____
_____
_____
_____

YEAR _____

_____
_____
_____
_____

YEAR _____

_____
_____
_____
_____

YEAR _____

_____
_____
_____
_____

YEAR _____

_____
_____
_____
_____

May

19

What are you saving money for right now?

YEAR _____

_____
_____
_____
_____

YEAR _____

_____
_____
_____
_____

YEAR _____

_____
_____
_____
_____

YEAR _____

_____
_____
_____
_____

YEAR _____

_____
_____
_____
_____

May

20

What was your last DIY project?

YEAR _____

_____
_____
_____
_____

YEAR _____

_____
_____
_____
_____

YEAR _____

_____
_____
_____
_____

YEAR _____

_____
_____
_____
_____

YEAR _____

_____
_____
_____
_____

May

21

A luxury you wish you had.

YEAR _____

_____
_____
_____
_____

YEAR _____

_____
_____
_____
_____

YEAR _____

_____
_____
_____
_____

YEAR _____

_____
_____
_____
_____

YEAR _____

_____
_____
_____
_____

May

22

Any sport you would like to try?

YEAR _____

_____
_____
_____
_____

YEAR _____

_____
_____
_____
_____

YEAR _____

_____
_____
_____
_____

YEAR _____

_____
_____
_____
_____

YEAR _____

_____
_____
_____
_____

May
23

A song that reminds you of your mother.

YEAR _____

_____
_____
_____
_____

YEAR _____

_____
_____
_____
_____

YEAR _____

_____
_____
_____
_____

YEAR _____

_____
_____
_____
_____

YEAR _____

_____
_____
_____
_____

May

24

Your favorite cool weather outfit.

YEAR _____
_____
_____
_____
_____

YEAR _____
_____
_____
_____
_____

YEAR _____
_____
_____
_____
_____

YEAR _____
_____
_____
_____
_____

YEAR _____
_____
_____
_____
_____

May

25

How is your health?

YEAR_____

_____
_____
_____
_____

YEAR_____

_____
_____
_____
_____

YEAR_____

_____
_____
_____
_____

YEAR_____

_____
_____
_____
_____

YEAR_____

_____
_____
_____
_____

May
26

How many hours of sleep did you get last night?

YEAR _____

_____

_____

_____

_____

YEAR _____

_____

_____

_____

_____

YEAR _____

_____

_____

_____

_____

YEAR _____

_____

_____

_____

_____

YEAR _____

_____

_____

_____

_____

May

27

A new skill you have learned.

YEAR_____

_____
_____
_____
_____

YEAR_____

_____
_____
_____
_____

YEAR_____

_____
_____
_____
_____

YEAR_____

_____
_____
_____
_____

YEAR_____

_____
_____
_____
_____

May

28

Share a childhood memory.

YEAR _____

_____

_____

_____

_____

YEAR _____

_____

_____

_____

_____

YEAR _____

_____

_____

_____

_____

YEAR _____

_____

_____

_____

_____

YEAR _____

_____

_____

_____

_____

May

29

Morning or Evening?

YEAR _____

_____
_____
_____
_____

YEAR _____

_____
_____
_____
_____

YEAR _____

_____
_____
_____
_____

YEAR _____

_____
_____
_____
_____

YEAR _____

_____
_____
_____
_____

May

30

What is your opinion on Terrorism?

YEAR _____

_____

_____

_____

_____

YEAR _____

_____

_____

_____

_____

YEAR _____

_____

_____

_____

_____

YEAR _____

_____

_____

_____

_____

YEAR _____

_____

_____

_____

_____

May

31

Cats or Dogs?

YEAR _____

_____
_____
_____
_____

YEAR _____

_____
_____
_____
_____

YEAR _____

_____
_____
_____
_____

YEAR _____

_____
_____
_____
_____

YEAR _____

_____
_____
_____
_____

June

1

A recent surprise.

YEAR _____

_____
_____
_____
_____

YEAR _____

_____
_____
_____
_____

YEAR _____

_____
_____
_____
_____

YEAR _____

_____
_____
_____
_____

YEAR _____

_____
_____
_____
_____

June

2

3 things you need to do more often.

YEAR_____
_____
_____
_____
_____

YEAR_____
_____
_____
_____
_____

YEAR_____
_____
_____
_____
_____

YEAR_____
_____
_____
_____
_____

YEAR_____
_____
_____
_____
_____

June

3

When did you last feel truly alive?

YEAR _____

_____
_____
_____
_____

YEAR _____

_____
_____
_____
_____

YEAR _____

_____
_____
_____
_____

YEAR _____

_____
_____
_____
_____

YEAR _____

_____
_____
_____
_____

June

4

Your good deeds for today.

YEAR _____

_____
_____
_____
_____

YEAR _____

_____
_____
_____
_____

YEAR _____

_____
_____
_____
_____

YEAR _____

_____
_____
_____
_____

YEAR _____

_____
_____
_____
_____

June

5

If your body could talk, what would it say to you?

YEAR _____

_____

_____

_____

_____

YEAR _____

_____

_____

_____

_____

YEAR _____

_____

_____

_____

_____

YEAR _____

_____

_____

_____

_____

YEAR _____

_____

_____

_____

_____

June

6

Pork or Beef?

YEAR _____

_____

_____

_____

_____

YEAR _____

_____

_____

_____

_____

YEAR _____

_____

_____

_____

_____

YEAR _____

_____

_____

_____

_____

YEAR _____

_____

_____

_____

_____

June

7

Write a short letter to someone you need to forgive.

YEAR _____

_____

_____

_____

_____

YEAR _____

_____

_____

_____

_____

YEAR _____

_____

_____

_____

_____

YEAR _____

_____

_____

_____

_____

YEAR _____

_____

_____

_____

_____

June

8

What was the hardest part about growing up?

YEAR _____

_____
_____
_____
_____

YEAR _____

_____
_____
_____
_____

YEAR _____

_____
_____
_____
_____

YEAR _____

_____
_____
_____
_____

YEAR _____

_____
_____
_____
_____

June

9

Any short-term goal you have reached this year?

YEAR_____

_____
_____
_____
_____

YEAR_____

_____
_____
_____
_____

YEAR_____

_____
_____
_____
_____

YEAR_____

_____
_____
_____
_____

YEAR_____

_____
_____
_____
_____

June

10

What did you buy today?

YEAR _____

_____
_____
_____
_____

YEAR _____

_____
_____
_____
_____

YEAR _____

_____
_____
_____
_____

YEAR _____

_____
_____
_____
_____

YEAR _____

_____
_____
_____
_____

June

11

When did you last show resilience?

YEAR _____

_____
_____
_____
_____

YEAR _____

_____
_____
_____
_____

YEAR _____

_____
_____
_____
_____

YEAR _____

_____
_____
_____
_____

YEAR _____

_____
_____
_____
_____

June

12

Who or what do you long for?

YEAR _____

_____
_____
_____
_____

YEAR _____

_____
_____
_____
_____

YEAR _____

_____
_____
_____
_____

YEAR _____

_____
_____
_____
_____

YEAR _____

_____
_____
_____
_____

June

13

Your victories of the past week.

YEAR _____
_____
_____
_____
_____

YEAR _____
_____
_____
_____
_____

YEAR _____
_____
_____
_____
_____

YEAR _____
_____
_____
_____
_____

YEAR _____
_____
_____
_____
_____

June

14

Have you grown spiritually? How do you say so?

YEAR _____

_____
_____
_____
_____

YEAR _____

_____
_____
_____
_____

YEAR _____

_____
_____
_____
_____

YEAR _____

_____
_____
_____
_____

YEAR _____

_____
_____
_____
_____

June

15

If you have a $1000 gift card,
what would you spend it on?

YEAR _____
_____
_____
_____
_____

YEAR _____
_____
_____
_____
_____

YEAR _____
_____
_____
_____
_____

YEAR _____
_____
_____
_____
_____

YEAR _____
_____
_____
_____
_____

June

16

The next book you want to read.

YEAR _____

_____
_____
_____
_____

YEAR _____

_____
_____
_____
_____

YEAR _____

_____
_____
_____
_____

YEAR _____

_____
_____
_____
_____

YEAR _____

_____
_____
_____
_____

June

17

If your life is a song, what song would it be?

YEAR_____

_____

_____

_____

_____

YEAR_____

_____

_____

_____

_____

YEAR_____

_____

_____

_____

_____

YEAR_____

_____

_____

_____

_____

YEAR_____

_____

_____

_____

_____

June

18

Your favorite musician.

YEAR _____

_____
_____
_____
_____

YEAR _____

_____
_____
_____
_____

YEAR _____

_____
_____
_____
_____

YEAR _____

_____
_____
_____
_____

YEAR _____

_____
_____
_____
_____

June

19

What is the most important thing you need to do today?

YEAR _____

_____
_____
_____
_____

YEAR _____

_____
_____
_____
_____

YEAR _____

_____
_____
_____
_____

YEAR _____

_____
_____
_____
_____

YEAR _____

_____
_____
_____
_____

June

20

What is the driving force in your life right now?

YEAR _____

_____
_____
_____
_____

YEAR _____

_____
_____
_____
_____

YEAR _____

_____
_____
_____
_____

YEAR _____

_____
_____
_____
_____

YEAR _____

_____
_____
_____
_____

June

21

iPhone or Samsung?

YEAR _____
_____
_____
_____
_____

YEAR _____
_____
_____
_____
_____

YEAR _____
_____
_____
_____
_____

YEAR _____
_____
_____
_____
_____

YEAR _____
_____
_____
_____
_____

June

22

What fears did you have this week?

YEAR _____

_____
_____
_____
_____

YEAR _____

_____
_____
_____
_____

YEAR _____

_____
_____
_____
_____

YEAR _____

_____
_____
_____
_____

YEAR _____

_____
_____
_____
_____

June

23

Who was the last person you kissed?

YEAR _____

_____
_____
_____
_____

YEAR _____

_____
_____
_____
_____

YEAR _____

_____
_____
_____
_____

YEAR _____

_____
_____
_____
_____

YEAR _____

_____
_____
_____
_____

June

If you could read one person's mind,
whose mind would you read and why?

YEAR _____

_____
_____
_____
_____

YEAR _____

_____
_____
_____
_____

YEAR _____

_____
_____
_____
_____

YEAR _____

_____
_____
_____
_____

YEAR _____

_____
_____
_____
_____

June

25

Favorite room in your house.

YEAR _____

_____
_____
_____
_____

YEAR _____

_____
_____
_____
_____

YEAR _____

_____
_____
_____
_____

YEAR _____

_____
_____
_____
_____

YEAR _____

_____
_____
_____
_____

June

26

You dad's favorite saying.

YEAR_____

_____
_____
_____
_____

YEAR_____

_____
_____
_____
_____

YEAR_____

_____
_____
_____
_____

YEAR_____

_____
_____
_____
_____

YEAR_____

_____
_____
_____
_____

June

27

Best meal you have cooked last week.

YEAR _____

_____

_____

_____

_____

YEAR _____

_____

_____

_____

_____

YEAR _____

_____

_____

_____

_____

YEAR _____

_____

_____

_____

_____

YEAR _____

_____

_____

_____

_____

June

28

A song that made you sad.

YEAR_____

_____
_____
_____
_____

YEAR_____

_____
_____
_____
_____

YEAR_____

_____
_____
_____
_____

YEAR_____

_____
_____
_____
_____

YEAR_____

_____
_____
_____
_____

June

29

Do you believe in miracles?

YEAR _____

_____
_____
_____
_____

YEAR _____

_____
_____
_____
_____

YEAR _____

_____
_____
_____
_____

YEAR _____

_____
_____
_____
_____

YEAR _____

_____
_____
_____
_____

June

30

Who changed you for the better?

YEAR _____

_____
_____
_____
_____

YEAR _____

_____
_____
_____
_____

YEAR _____

_____
_____
_____
_____

YEAR _____

_____
_____
_____
_____

YEAR _____

_____
_____
_____
_____

July

1

A time you pulled an all-nighter.

YEAR _____

_____

_____

_____

_____

YEAR _____

_____

_____

_____

_____

YEAR _____

_____

_____

_____

_____

YEAR _____

_____

_____

_____

_____

YEAR _____

_____

_____

_____

_____

July

2

What is your favorite sport to watch?

YEAR _____

_____

_____

_____

_____

YEAR _____

_____

_____

_____

_____

YEAR _____

_____

_____

_____

_____

YEAR _____

_____

_____

_____

_____

YEAR _____

_____

_____

_____

_____

July

3

Apple or Banana?

YEAR _____

_____
_____
_____
_____

YEAR _____

_____
_____
_____
_____

YEAR _____

_____
_____
_____
_____

YEAR _____

_____
_____
_____
_____

YEAR _____

_____
_____
_____
_____

July

4

Any book you are reading right now?

YEAR _____

_____

_____

_____

_____

YEAR _____

_____

_____

_____

_____

YEAR _____

_____

_____

_____

_____

YEAR _____

_____

_____

_____

_____

YEAR _____

_____

_____

_____

_____

July

5

What is your opinion on Fixed Marriages?

YEAR_____

_____
_____
_____
_____

YEAR_____

_____
_____
_____
_____

YEAR_____

_____
_____
_____
_____

YEAR_____

_____
_____
_____
_____

YEAR_____

_____
_____
_____
_____

July

6

What life lessons did you learn the hard way?

YEAR _____

_____

_____

_____

_____

YEAR _____

_____

_____

_____

_____

YEAR _____

_____

_____

_____

_____

YEAR _____

_____

_____

_____

_____

YEAR _____

_____

_____

_____

_____

July

7

What would you teach young people nowadays?

YEAR _____
_____
_____
_____
_____

YEAR _____
_____
_____
_____
_____

YEAR _____
_____
_____
_____
_____

YEAR _____
_____
_____
_____
_____

YEAR _____
_____
_____
_____
_____

July

8

What is your belief which many people disagree with?

YEAR_____

_____
_____
_____
_____

YEAR_____

_____
_____
_____
_____

YEAR_____

_____
_____
_____
_____

YEAR_____

_____
_____
_____
_____

YEAR_____

_____
_____
_____
_____

July

9

Have you done anything worth remembering lately?

YEAR _____

_____
_____
_____
_____

YEAR _____

_____
_____
_____
_____

YEAR _____

_____
_____
_____
_____

YEAR _____

_____
_____
_____
_____

YEAR _____

_____
_____
_____
_____

July

10

Write something about an influential friend.

YEAR _____

_____

_____

_____

_____

YEAR _____

_____

_____

_____

_____

YEAR _____

_____

_____

_____

_____

YEAR _____

_____

_____

_____

_____

YEAR _____

_____

_____

_____

_____

July

11

What traits do you admire in your parents?

YEAR _____

_____

_____

_____

_____

YEAR _____

_____

_____

_____

_____

YEAR _____

_____

_____

_____

_____

YEAR _____

_____

_____

_____

_____

YEAR _____

_____

_____

_____

_____

July

12

What does freedom mean?

YEAR _____

_____
_____
_____
_____

YEAR _____

_____
_____
_____
_____

YEAR _____

_____
_____
_____
_____

YEAR _____

_____
_____
_____
_____

YEAR _____

_____
_____
_____
_____

July

13

Were you creative today?

YEAR _____

_____
_____
_____
_____

YEAR _____

_____
_____
_____
_____

YEAR _____

_____
_____
_____
_____

YEAR _____

_____
_____
_____
_____

YEAR _____

_____
_____
_____
_____

July

14

How is your financial status?

YEAR _____

_____
_____
_____
_____

YEAR _____

_____
_____
_____
_____

YEAR _____

_____
_____
_____
_____

YEAR _____

_____
_____
_____
_____

YEAR _____

_____
_____
_____
_____

July

15

A new friend.

YEAR_____

_____
_____
_____
_____

YEAR_____

_____
_____
_____
_____

YEAR_____

_____
_____
_____
_____

YEAR_____

_____
_____
_____
_____

YEAR_____

_____
_____
_____
_____

July

16

List the cards in your wallet.

YEAR _____

_____

_____

_____

_____

YEAR _____

_____

_____

_____

_____

YEAR _____

_____

_____

_____

_____

YEAR _____

_____

_____

_____

_____

YEAR _____

_____

_____

_____

_____

July

17

How many sit-ups can you do now?

YEAR _____

_____

_____

_____

_____

YEAR _____

_____

_____

_____

_____

YEAR _____

_____

_____

_____

_____

YEAR _____

_____

_____

_____

_____

YEAR _____

_____

_____

_____

_____

July

18

What was the most flattering thing
you were told this week?

YEAR _____

_____
_____
_____
_____

YEAR _____

_____
_____
_____
_____

YEAR _____

_____
_____
_____
_____

YEAR _____

_____
_____
_____
_____

YEAR _____

_____
_____
_____
_____

July

19

What projects are you currently working on?

YEAR _____

_____
_____
_____
_____

YEAR _____

_____
_____
_____
_____

YEAR _____

_____
_____
_____
_____

YEAR _____

_____
_____
_____
_____

YEAR _____

_____
_____
_____
_____

July

20

Intelligence or Compassion?

YEAR _____

_____
_____
_____
_____

YEAR _____

_____
_____
_____
_____

YEAR _____

_____
_____
_____
_____

YEAR _____

_____
_____
_____
_____

YEAR _____

_____
_____
_____
_____

July

21

The first thing you thought about
when you woke up today.

YEAR _____

_____
_____
_____
_____

YEAR _____

_____
_____
_____
_____

YEAR _____

_____
_____
_____
_____

YEAR _____

_____
_____
_____
_____

YEAR _____

_____
_____
_____
_____

July

22

Do you crying is a sign of weakness? Why?

YEAR _____

_____

_____

_____

_____

YEAR _____

_____

_____

_____

_____

YEAR _____

_____

_____

_____

_____

YEAR _____

_____

_____

_____

_____

YEAR _____

_____

_____

_____

_____

July

23

When was the last time you told someone off?

YEAR _____

_____
,_____
_____
_____

YEAR _____

_____
_____
_____
_____

YEAR _____

_____
_____
_____
_____

YEAR _____

_____
_____
_____
_____

YEAR _____

_____
_____
_____
_____

July

24

If you could donate in a charity,
where would you donate to and why?

YEAR _____

_____

_____

_____

_____

YEAR _____

_____

_____

_____

_____

YEAR _____

_____

_____

_____

_____

YEAR _____

_____

_____

_____

_____

YEAR _____

_____

_____

_____

_____

July

25

Your beliefs on Religion.

YEAR _____

_____
_____
_____
_____

YEAR _____

_____
_____
_____
_____

YEAR _____

_____
_____
_____
_____

YEAR _____

_____
_____
_____
_____

YEAR _____

_____
_____
_____
_____

July

26

A party you last attended.

YEAR _____

_____
_____
_____
_____

YEAR _____

_____
_____
_____
_____

YEAR _____

_____
_____
_____
_____

YEAR _____

_____
_____
_____
_____

YEAR _____

_____
_____
_____
_____

July

27

What was in your email today?

YEAR _____

_____
_____
_____
_____

YEAR _____

_____
_____
_____
_____

YEAR _____

_____
_____
_____
_____

YEAR _____

_____
_____
_____
_____

YEAR _____

_____
_____
_____
_____

July

28

How many friends do you have on Facebook or Twitter?

YEAR _____

_____
_____
_____
_____

YEAR _____

_____
_____
_____
_____

YEAR _____

_____
_____
_____
_____

YEAR _____

_____
_____
_____
_____

YEAR _____

_____
_____
_____
_____

July

29

Your comfort food.

YEAR _____

_____

_____

_____

_____

YEAR _____

_____

_____

_____

_____

YEAR _____

_____

_____

_____

_____

YEAR _____

_____

_____

_____

_____

YEAR _____

_____

_____

_____

_____

July

30

10 things that you were grateful for this month.

YEAR _____

_____
_____
_____
_____

YEAR _____

_____
_____
_____
_____

YEAR _____

_____
_____
_____
_____

YEAR _____

_____
_____
_____
_____

YEAR _____

_____
_____
_____
_____

July

31

Beauty or Brains?

YEAR _____

_____

_____

_____

_____

YEAR _____

_____

_____

_____

_____

YEAR _____

_____

_____

_____

_____

YEAR _____

_____

_____

_____

_____

YEAR _____

_____

_____

_____

_____

August

1

What color makes you think of happiness?

YEAR _____

_____
_____
_____
_____

YEAR _____

_____
_____
_____
_____

YEAR _____

_____
_____
_____
_____

YEAR _____

_____
_____
_____
_____

YEAR _____

_____
_____
_____
_____

August

2

Your recent favorite restaurant.

YEAR_____

_____
_____
_____
_____

YEAR_____

_____
_____
_____
_____

YEAR_____

_____
_____
_____
_____

YEAR_____

_____
_____
_____
_____

YEAR_____

_____
_____
_____
_____

August

3

Black or White?

YEAR_____

_____
_____
_____
_____

YEAR_____

_____
_____
_____
_____

YEAR_____

_____
_____
_____
_____

YEAR_____

_____
_____
_____
_____

YEAR_____

_____
_____
_____
_____

August
4

What can you do today
that you were not capable of a year ago?

YEAR _____

_____
_____
_____
_____

YEAR _____

_____
_____
_____
_____

YEAR _____

_____
_____
_____
_____

YEAR _____

_____
_____
_____
_____

YEAR _____

_____
_____
_____
_____

August

5

Describe your mood today.

YEAR _____
_____
_____
_____
_____

YEAR _____
_____
_____
_____
_____

YEAR _____
_____
_____
_____
_____

YEAR _____
_____
_____
_____
_____

YEAR _____
_____
_____
_____
_____

August

6

3 things you need to do less often.

YEAR _____

_____
_____
_____
_____

YEAR _____

_____
_____
_____
_____

YEAR _____

_____
_____
_____
_____

YEAR _____

_____
_____
_____
_____

YEAR _____

_____
_____
_____
_____

August

7

The last person you said "I love you" to.

YEAR _____

_____
_____
_____
_____

YEAR _____

_____
_____
_____
_____

YEAR _____

_____
_____
_____
_____

YEAR _____

_____
_____
_____
_____

YEAR _____

_____
_____
_____
_____

August

8

Would you forgive betrayal?

YEAR _____

_____
_____
_____
_____

YEAR _____

_____
_____
_____
_____

YEAR _____

_____
_____
_____
_____

YEAR _____

_____
_____
_____
_____

YEAR _____

_____
_____
_____
_____

August

9

Which activities make you lose track of time?

YEAR _____

_____

_____

_____

_____

YEAR _____

_____

_____

_____

_____

YEAR _____

_____

_____

_____

_____

YEAR _____

_____

_____

_____

_____

YEAR _____

_____

_____

_____

_____

August

10

Your morning routine.

YEAR _____

_____
_____
_____
_____

YEAR _____

_____
_____
_____
_____

YEAR _____

_____
_____
_____
_____

YEAR _____

_____
_____
_____
_____

YEAR _____

_____
_____
_____
_____

August

11

Are you insecure? Why?

YEAR _____

_____
_____
_____
_____

YEAR _____

_____
_____
_____
_____

YEAR _____

_____
_____
_____
_____

YEAR _____

_____
_____
_____
_____

YEAR _____

_____
_____
_____
_____

August

12

Husky or Pug?

YEAR _____

_____
_____
_____
_____

YEAR _____

_____
_____
_____
_____

YEAR _____

_____
_____
_____
_____

YEAR _____

_____
_____
_____
_____

YEAR _____

_____
_____
_____
_____

August

13

Write a short letter to your past self.

YEAR _____

_____
_____
_____
_____

YEAR _____

_____
_____
_____
_____

YEAR _____

_____
_____
_____
_____

YEAR _____

_____
_____
_____
_____

YEAR _____

_____
_____
_____
_____

August

14

Who made you happy today?

YEAR _____

_____
_____
_____
_____

YEAR _____

_____
_____
_____
_____

YEAR _____

_____
_____
_____
_____

YEAR _____

_____
_____
_____
_____

YEAR _____

_____
_____
_____
_____

August
15

Do you often compare yourself to others? Why?

YEAR _____

YEAR _____

YEAR _____

YEAR _____

YEAR _____

August

16

Your best accomplishment today.

YEAR _____

_____
_____
_____
_____

YEAR _____

_____
_____
_____
_____

YEAR _____

_____
_____
_____
_____

YEAR _____

_____
_____
_____
_____

YEAR _____

_____
_____
_____
_____

August

17

Your ideal pamper routine.

YEAR_____

_____

_____

_____

_____

YEAR_____

_____

_____

_____

_____

YEAR_____

_____

_____

_____

_____

YEAR_____

_____

_____

_____

_____

YEAR_____

_____

_____

_____

_____

August

18

The best dream you have ever had.

YEAR _____

_____
_____
_____
_____

YEAR _____

_____
_____
_____
_____

YEAR _____

_____
_____
_____
_____

YEAR _____

_____
_____
_____
_____

YEAR _____

_____
_____
_____
_____

August

19

Money or Love?

YEAR _____

_____
_____
_____
_____

YEAR _____

_____
_____
_____
_____

YEAR _____

_____
_____
_____
_____

YEAR _____

_____
_____
_____
_____

YEAR _____

_____
_____
_____
_____

August

20

What has challenged your morals lately?

YEAR _____

_____

_____

_____

_____

YEAR _____

_____

_____

_____

_____

YEAR _____

_____

_____

_____

_____

YEAR _____

_____

_____

_____

_____

YEAR _____

_____

_____

_____

_____

August

21

What makes you anxious?

YEAR_____

_____
_____
_____
_____

YEAR_____

_____
_____
_____
_____

YEAR_____

_____
_____
_____
_____

YEAR_____

_____
_____
_____
_____

YEAR_____

_____
_____
_____
_____

August

22

When you are 60 years old,
what will matter to you the most and why?

YEAR_____

_____
_____
_____
_____

YEAR_____

_____
_____
_____
_____

YEAR_____

_____
_____
_____
_____

YEAR_____

_____
_____
_____
_____

YEAR_____

_____
_____
_____
_____

August

23

One quality you would never want to change
about yourself and why.

YEAR _____

_____

_____

_____

_____

YEAR _____

_____

_____

_____

_____

YEAR _____

_____

_____

_____

_____

YEAR _____

_____

_____

_____

_____

YEAR _____

_____

_____

_____

_____

August

24

Your best talent.

YEAR _____

_____
_____
_____
_____

YEAR _____

_____
_____
_____
_____

YEAR _____

_____
_____
_____
_____

YEAR _____

_____
_____
_____
_____

YEAR _____

_____
_____
_____
_____

August

25

What hardships have you overcome lately?

YEAR _____

_____
_____
_____
_____

YEAR _____

_____
_____
_____
_____

YEAR _____

_____
_____
_____
_____

YEAR _____

_____
_____
_____
_____

YEAR _____

_____
_____
_____
_____

August

26

Ability to fly or mind-reader?

YEAR_____

_____
_____
_____
_____

YEAR_____

_____
_____
_____
_____

YEAR_____

_____
_____
_____
_____

YEAR_____

_____
_____
_____
_____

YEAR_____

_____
_____
_____
_____

August

27

Who was the first person you saw today?

YEAR _____

_____

_____

_____

_____

YEAR _____

_____

_____

_____

_____

YEAR _____

_____

_____

_____

_____

YEAR _____

_____

_____

_____

_____

YEAR _____

_____

_____

_____

_____

August

28

What is worth fighting for?

YEAR _____

_____

_____

_____

_____

YEAR _____

_____

_____

_____

_____

YEAR _____

_____

_____

_____

_____

YEAR _____

_____

_____

_____

_____

YEAR _____

_____

_____

_____

_____

August

29

How much money is in your wallet right now?

YEAR _____

_____
_____
_____
_____

YEAR _____

_____
_____
_____
_____

YEAR _____

_____
_____
_____
_____

YEAR _____

_____
_____
_____
_____

YEAR _____

_____
_____
_____
_____

August

30

Were you a positive or negative person today?

YEAR _____

_____
_____
_____
_____

YEAR _____

_____
_____
_____
_____

YEAR _____

_____
_____
_____
_____

YEAR _____

_____
_____
_____
_____

YEAR _____

_____
_____
_____
_____

August

31

How did you use your time wisely today?

YEAR _____

_____

_____

_____

_____

YEAR _____

_____

_____

_____

_____

YEAR _____

_____

_____

_____

_____

YEAR _____

_____

_____

_____

_____

YEAR _____

_____

_____

_____

_____

September

1

Who do you love unconditionally?

YEAR _____

_____

_____

_____

_____

YEAR _____

_____

_____

_____

_____

YEAR _____

_____

_____

_____

_____

YEAR _____

_____

_____

_____

_____

YEAR _____

_____

_____

_____

_____

September

2

Your favorite pair of shoes you own now.

YEAR _____

_____
_____
_____
_____

YEAR _____

_____
_____
_____
_____

YEAR _____

_____
_____
_____
_____

YEAR _____

_____
_____
_____
_____

YEAR _____

_____
_____
_____
_____

September

3

Dancing or Singing?

YEAR _____

_____
_____
_____
_____

YEAR _____

_____
_____
_____
_____

YEAR _____

_____
_____
_____
_____

YEAR _____

_____
_____
_____
_____

YEAR _____

_____
_____
_____
_____

September

4

A movie that reminds you of your father.

YEAR _____

_____

_____

_____

_____

YEAR _____

_____

_____

_____

_____

YEAR _____

_____

_____

_____

_____

YEAR _____

_____

_____

_____

_____

YEAR _____

_____

_____

_____

_____

September

5

Share a secret thought.

YEAR _____

_____
_____
_____
_____

YEAR _____

_____
_____
_____
_____

YEAR _____

_____
_____
_____
_____

YEAR _____

_____
_____
_____
_____

YEAR _____

_____
_____
_____
_____

September

6

Hot coffee or Iced coffee?

YEAR _____

_____

_____

_____

_____

YEAR _____

_____

_____

_____

_____

YEAR _____

_____

_____

_____

_____

YEAR _____

_____

_____

_____

_____

YEAR _____

_____

_____

_____

_____

September

7

What made you feel tired today?

YEAR _____

_____

_____

_____

_____

YEAR _____

_____

_____

_____

_____

YEAR _____

_____

_____

_____

_____

YEAR _____

_____

_____

_____

_____

YEAR _____

_____

_____

_____

_____

September

8

What is your super power?

YEAR _____

_____
_____
_____
_____

YEAR _____

_____
_____
_____
_____

YEAR _____

_____
_____
_____
_____

YEAR _____

_____
_____
_____
_____

YEAR _____

_____
_____
_____
_____

September

9

List your pets.

YEAR _____
_____
_____
_____
_____

YEAR _____
_____
_____
_____
_____

YEAR _____
_____
_____
_____
_____

YEAR _____
_____
_____
_____
_____

YEAR _____
_____
_____
_____
_____

September

10

Your struggles of the past week.

YEAR _____

_____
_____
_____
_____

YEAR _____

_____
_____
_____
_____

YEAR _____

_____
_____
_____
_____

YEAR _____

_____
_____
_____
_____

YEAR _____

_____
_____
_____
_____

September

11

How good do you feel about yourself today and why?

YEAR _____

_____
_____
_____
_____

YEAR _____

_____
_____
_____
_____

YEAR _____

_____
_____
_____
_____

YEAR _____

_____
_____
_____
_____

YEAR _____

_____
_____
_____
_____

September

12

What made you sad recently?

YEAR _____

_____
_____
_____
_____

YEAR _____

_____
_____
_____
_____

YEAR _____

_____
_____
_____
_____

YEAR _____

_____
_____
_____
_____

YEAR _____

_____
_____
_____
_____

September

13

If you could step into somebody's dream,
whose dream would you invade and why?

YEAR _____

_____
_____
_____
_____

YEAR _____

_____
_____
_____
_____

YEAR _____

_____
_____
_____
_____

YEAR _____

_____
_____
_____
_____

YEAR _____

_____
_____
_____
_____

September

14

Is social media one giant bully? Why?

YEAR_____

_____
_____
_____
_____

YEAR_____

_____
_____
_____
_____

YEAR_____

_____
_____
_____
_____

YEAR_____

_____
_____
_____
_____

YEAR_____

_____
_____
_____
_____

September

15

Things you did when you were last drunk.

YEAR _____

_____
_____
_____
_____

YEAR _____

_____
_____
_____
_____

YEAR _____

_____
_____
_____
_____

YEAR _____

_____
_____
_____
_____

YEAR _____

_____
_____
_____
_____

September

16

Are you more worried about doing things right,
or doing the right things?

YEAR _____

_____
_____
_____
_____

YEAR _____

_____
_____
_____
_____

YEAR _____

_____
_____
_____
_____

YEAR _____

_____
_____
_____

YEAR _____

_____
_____
_____
_____

September

17

Summer or Fall?

YEAR _____

_____
_____
_____
_____

YEAR _____

_____
_____
_____
_____

YEAR _____

_____
_____
_____
_____

YEAR _____

_____
_____
_____
_____

YEAR _____

_____
_____
_____
_____

September

18

Are you holding a grudge now? With whom and why?

YEAR _____

_____
_____
_____
_____

YEAR _____

_____
_____
_____
_____

YEAR _____

_____
_____
_____
_____

YEAR _____

_____
_____
_____
_____

YEAR _____

_____
_____
_____
_____

September

19

A time you strived to prove yourself to someone
and how that affected you.

YEAR _____

_____
_____
_____
_____

YEAR _____

_____
_____
_____
_____

YEAR _____

_____
_____
_____
_____

YEAR _____

_____
_____
_____
_____

YEAR _____

_____
_____
_____
_____

September

Think about the happiest person you have ever met.
What can you learn about him/her?

YEAR _____

_____

_____

_____

_____

YEAR _____

_____

_____

_____

_____

YEAR _____

_____

_____

_____

_____

YEAR _____

_____

_____

_____

_____

YEAR _____

_____

_____

_____

_____

September

21

What was your dream job when you were a child?

YEAR _____

_____

_____

_____

_____

YEAR _____

_____

_____

_____

_____

YEAR _____

_____

_____

_____

_____

YEAR _____

_____

_____

_____

_____

YEAR _____

_____

_____

_____

_____

September

22

What did you eat for breakfast today?

YEAR _____

_____
_____
_____
_____

YEAR _____

_____
_____
_____
_____

YEAR _____

_____
_____
_____
_____

YEAR _____

_____
_____
_____
_____

YEAR _____

_____
_____
_____
_____

September

23

If you were Aladdin and you have 3 wishes,
what would be your wish??

YEAR _____

_____
_____
_____
_____

YEAR _____

_____
_____
_____
_____

YEAR _____

_____
_____
_____
_____

YEAR _____

_____
_____
_____
_____

YEAR _____

_____
_____
_____
_____

September

24

Does Love hurt? Explain why.

YEAR _____
_____
_____
_____
_____

YEAR _____
_____
_____
_____
_____

YEAR _____
_____
_____
_____
_____

YEAR _____
_____
_____
_____
_____

YEAR _____
_____
_____
_____
_____

September

25

Something big or small you did today
that you were proud of.

YEAR _____

_____
_____
_____
_____

YEAR _____

_____
_____
_____
_____

YEAR _____

_____
_____
_____
_____

YEAR _____

_____
_____
_____
_____

YEAR _____

_____
_____
_____
_____

September

26

Japan or South Korea?

YEAR_____

_____
_____
_____
_____

YEAR_____

_____
_____
_____
_____

YEAR_____

_____
_____
_____
_____

YEAR_____

_____
_____
_____
_____

YEAR_____

_____
_____
_____
_____

September

27

Would you do Bungee Jumping for $1,000?

YEAR _____

_____
_____
_____
_____

YEAR _____

_____
_____
_____
_____

YEAR _____

_____
_____
_____
_____

YEAR _____

_____
_____
_____
_____

YEAR _____

_____
_____
_____
_____

September

28

Things you said the last time you were angry.

YEAR _____

_____
_____
_____
_____

YEAR _____

_____
_____
_____
_____

YEAR _____

_____
_____
_____
_____

YEAR _____

_____
_____
_____
_____

YEAR _____

_____
_____
_____
_____

September

29

What would you do if you heard people
gossiping about you?

YEAR _____

_____
_____
_____
_____

YEAR _____

_____
_____
_____
_____

YEAR _____

_____
_____
_____
_____

YEAR _____

_____
_____
_____
_____

YEAR _____

_____
_____
_____
_____

September

30

Your thoughts about depression and suicide.

YEAR _____

_____
_____
_____
_____

YEAR _____

_____
_____
_____
_____

YEAR _____

_____
_____
_____
_____

YEAR _____

_____
_____
_____
_____

YEAR _____

_____
_____
_____
_____

October

1

Rabbit or Turtle?

YEAR _____

_____
_____
_____
_____

YEAR _____

_____
_____
_____
_____

YEAR _____

_____
_____
_____
_____

YEAR _____

_____
_____
_____
_____

YEAR _____

_____
_____
_____
_____

October

2

What change can I make today?

YEAR _____

_____

_____

_____

_____

YEAR _____

_____

_____

_____

_____

YEAR _____

_____

_____

_____

_____

YEAR _____

_____

_____

_____

_____

YEAR _____

_____

_____

_____

_____

October

3

What makes you feel inadequate?

YEAR _____

_____
_____
_____
_____

YEAR _____

_____
_____
_____
_____

YEAR _____

_____
_____
_____
_____

YEAR _____

_____
_____
_____
_____

YEAR _____

_____
_____
_____
_____

October

4

You mom's favorite saying.

YEAR _____

_____
_____
_____
_____

YEAR _____

_____
_____
_____
_____

YEAR _____

_____
_____
_____
_____

YEAR _____

_____
_____
_____
_____

YEAR _____

_____
_____
_____
_____

October

5

Write a short letter to your past self.

YEAR _____

_____
_____
_____
_____

YEAR _____

_____
_____
_____
_____

YEAR _____

_____
_____
_____
_____

YEAR _____

_____
_____
_____
_____

YEAR _____

_____
_____
_____
_____

October

6

What triggers your anxiety and how can you combat this?

YEAR _____

_____
_____
_____
_____

YEAR _____

_____
_____
_____
_____

YEAR _____

_____
_____
_____
_____

YEAR _____

_____
_____
_____
_____

YEAR _____

_____
_____
_____
_____

October

7

Fun memory of last week.

YEAR _____

_____
_____
_____
_____

YEAR _____

_____
_____
_____
_____

YEAR _____

_____
_____
_____
_____

YEAR _____

_____
_____
_____
_____

YEAR _____

_____
_____
_____
_____

October

8

What have you done for yourself lately?

YEAR _____

_____
_____
_____
_____

YEAR _____

_____
_____
_____
_____

YEAR _____

_____
_____
_____
_____

YEAR _____

_____
_____
_____
_____

YEAR _____

_____
_____
_____
_____

October

9

Do you believe that
you become what you think you are? Explain.

YEAR _____

_____
_____
_____
_____

YEAR _____

_____
_____
_____
_____

YEAR _____

_____
_____
_____
_____

YEAR _____

_____
_____
_____
_____

YEAR _____

_____
_____
_____
_____

October

10

How much did you improve this year?

YEAR _____

_____
_____
_____
_____

YEAR _____

_____
_____
_____
_____

YEAR _____

_____
_____
_____
_____

YEAR _____

_____
_____
_____
_____

YEAR _____

_____
_____
_____
_____

October

11

Gold or Silver?

YEAR_____

_____
_____
_____
_____

YEAR_____

_____
_____
_____
_____

YEAR_____

_____
_____
_____
_____

YEAR_____

_____
_____
_____
_____

YEAR_____

_____
_____
_____
_____

October

12

Today you should start believing in _____ .

YEAR _____

_____

_____

_____

_____

YEAR _____

_____

_____

_____

_____

YEAR _____

_____

_____

_____

_____

YEAR _____

_____

_____

_____

_____

YEAR _____

_____

_____

_____

_____

October

13

Are you more of an introvert or extrovert?

YEAR _____

_____
_____
_____
_____

YEAR _____

_____
_____
_____
_____

YEAR _____

_____
_____
_____
_____

YEAR _____

_____
_____
_____
_____

YEAR _____

_____
_____
_____
_____

October

14

A habit you just need to stop doing.

YEAR _____

_____
_____
_____
_____

YEAR _____

_____
_____
_____
_____

YEAR _____

_____
_____
_____
_____

YEAR _____

_____
_____
_____
_____

YEAR _____

_____
_____
_____
_____

October

15

What was the last thing that hurt you?

YEAR _____

_____

_____

_____

_____

YEAR _____

_____

_____

_____

_____

YEAR _____

_____

_____

_____

_____

YEAR _____

_____

_____

_____

_____

YEAR _____

_____

_____

_____

_____

October

16

If you could have any chef that will
prepare any meal for you, what would it be?

YEAR _____

_____

_____

_____

_____

YEAR _____

_____

_____

_____

_____

YEAR _____

_____

_____

_____

_____

YEAR _____

_____

_____

_____

_____

YEAR _____

_____

_____

_____

_____

October

17

Your favorite personality trait.

YEAR_____

_____
_____
_____
_____

YEAR_____

_____
_____
_____
_____

YEAR_____

_____
_____
_____
_____

YEAR_____

_____
_____
_____
_____

YEAR_____

_____
_____
_____
_____

October

18

Pop or Rock?

YEAR_____

_____
_____
_____
_____

YEAR_____

_____
_____
_____
_____

YEAR_____

_____
_____
_____
_____

YEAR_____

_____
_____
_____
_____

YEAR_____

_____
_____
_____
_____

October

19

Do you think it is important to be wealthy? Explain.

YEAR_____

_____
_____
_____
_____

YEAR_____

_____
_____
_____
_____

YEAR_____

_____
_____
_____
_____

YEAR_____

_____
_____
_____
_____

YEAR_____

_____
_____
_____
_____

October

20

Describe your kitchen.

YEAR _____

_____
_____
_____
_____

YEAR _____

_____
_____
_____
_____

YEAR _____

_____
_____
_____
_____

YEAR _____

_____
_____
_____
_____

YEAR _____

_____
_____
_____
_____

October

21

Write the words that you really need to hear now.

YEAR _____

_____
_____
_____
_____

YEAR _____

_____
_____
_____
_____

YEAR _____

_____
_____
_____
_____

YEAR _____

_____
_____
_____
_____

YEAR _____

_____
_____
_____
_____

October

22

An embarrassing moment in public in the past few weeks.

YEAR _____

_____

_____

_____

_____

YEAR _____

_____

_____

_____

_____

YEAR _____

_____

_____

_____

_____

YEAR _____

_____

_____

_____

_____

YEAR _____

_____

_____

_____

_____

October

23

Beginning or End?

YEAR _____

_____
_____
_____
_____

YEAR _____

_____
_____
_____
_____

YEAR _____

_____
_____
_____
_____

YEAR _____

_____
_____
_____
_____

YEAR _____

_____
_____
_____
_____

October

24

Are you more of a leader or a follower?

YEAR _____

_____
_____
_____
_____

YEAR _____

_____
_____
_____
_____

YEAR _____

_____
_____
_____
_____

YEAR _____

_____
_____
_____
_____

YEAR _____

_____
_____
_____
_____

October

25

What do you love about your current work?

YEAR _____

_____
_____
_____
_____

YEAR _____

_____
_____
_____
_____

YEAR _____

_____
_____
_____
_____

YEAR _____

_____
_____
_____
_____

YEAR _____

_____
_____
_____
_____

October

26

What do you hate about your current work?

YEAR_____

_____
_____
_____
_____

YEAR_____

_____
_____
_____
_____

YEAR_____

_____
_____
_____
_____

YEAR_____

_____
_____
_____
_____

YEAR_____

_____
_____
_____
_____

October

27

An important event that happened this month.

YEAR _____

_____
_____
_____
_____

YEAR _____

_____
_____
_____
_____

YEAR _____

_____
_____
_____
_____

YEAR _____

_____
_____
_____
_____

YEAR _____

_____
_____
_____
_____

October

28

Do you think life is harder or easier now? Why?

YEAR _____

_____

_____

_____

_____

YEAR _____

_____

_____

_____

_____

YEAR _____

_____

_____

_____

_____

YEAR _____

_____

_____

_____

_____

YEAR _____

_____

_____

_____

_____

October

29

Something you did recently
that you never thought you could.

YEAR _____

_____

_____

_____

_____

YEAR _____

_____

_____

_____

_____

YEAR _____

_____

_____

_____

_____

YEAR _____

_____

_____

_____

_____

YEAR _____

_____

_____

_____

_____

October

30

Aliens or Ghosts?

YEAR _____

_____
_____
_____
_____

YEAR _____

_____
_____
_____
_____

YEAR _____

_____
_____
_____
_____

YEAR _____

_____
_____
_____
_____

YEAR _____

_____
_____
_____
_____

October

31

Tricks or Treats?

YEAR_____

_____
_____
_____
_____

YEAR_____

_____
_____
_____
_____

YEAR_____

_____
_____
_____
_____

YEAR_____

_____
_____
_____
_____

YEAR_____

_____
_____
_____
_____

November

1

Your recent favorite horror movie.

YEAR _____

_____
_____
_____
_____

YEAR _____

_____
_____
_____
_____

YEAR _____

_____
_____
_____
_____

YEAR _____

_____
_____
_____
_____

YEAR _____

_____
_____
_____
_____

November

2

The last thing you thought about
before going to bed last night.

YEAR _____

_____
_____
_____
_____

YEAR _____

_____
_____
_____
_____

YEAR _____

_____
_____
_____
_____

YEAR _____

_____
_____
_____
_____

YEAR _____

_____
_____
_____
_____

November

3

Things you said when you last cried.

YEAR _____

_____

_____

_____

_____

YEAR _____

_____

_____

_____

_____

YEAR _____

_____

_____

_____

_____

YEAR _____

_____

_____

_____

_____

YEAR _____

_____

_____

_____

_____

November

4

Best joked you have ever played this year.

YEAR _____
_____
_____
_____
_____

YEAR _____
_____
_____
_____
_____

YEAR _____
_____
_____
_____
_____

YEAR _____
_____
_____
_____
_____

YEAR _____
_____
_____
_____
_____

November

5

Write a short letter to your future self.

YEAR _____

_____
_____
_____
_____

YEAR _____

_____
_____
_____
_____

YEAR _____

_____
_____
_____
_____

YEAR _____

_____
_____
_____
_____

YEAR _____

_____
_____
_____
_____

November

6

Math or Science?

YEAR _____

_____
_____
_____
_____

YEAR _____

_____
_____
_____
_____

YEAR _____

_____
_____
_____
_____

YEAR _____

_____
_____
_____
_____

YEAR _____

_____
_____
_____
_____

November

7

What world festivals would you like to attend?

YEAR _____

_____
_____
_____
_____

YEAR _____

_____
_____
_____
_____

YEAR _____

_____
_____
_____
_____

YEAR _____

_____
_____
_____
_____

YEAR _____

_____
_____
_____
_____

November

8

The next movie you want to see.

YEAR _____

_____
_____
_____
_____

YEAR _____

_____
_____
_____
_____

YEAR _____

_____
_____
_____
_____

YEAR _____

_____
_____
_____
_____

YEAR _____

_____
_____
_____
_____

November

9

There is no such thing as _____.

YEAR_____

_____
_____
_____
_____

YEAR_____

_____
_____
_____
_____

YEAR_____

_____
_____
_____
_____

YEAR_____

_____
_____
_____
_____

YEAR_____

_____
_____
_____
_____

November

10

Are you confident in your abilities now? Explain.

YEAR _____

_____

_____

_____

_____

YEAR _____

_____

_____

_____

_____

YEAR _____

_____

_____

_____

_____

YEAR _____

_____

_____

_____

_____

YEAR _____

_____

_____

_____

_____

November

11

What has troubled you lately?

YEAR _____

_____

_____

_____

_____

YEAR _____

_____

_____

_____

_____

YEAR _____

_____

_____

_____

_____

YEAR _____

_____

_____

_____

_____

YEAR _____

_____

_____

_____

_____

November

12

Rain or Snow?

YEAR _____

_____

_____

_____

_____

YEAR _____

_____

_____

_____

_____

YEAR _____

_____

_____

_____

_____

YEAR _____

_____

_____

_____

_____

YEAR _____

_____

_____

_____

_____

November

13

Do you think it is important to finish college?
Explain.

YEAR_____

_____
_____
_____
_____

YEAR_____

_____
_____
_____
_____

YEAR_____

_____
_____
_____
_____

YEAR_____

_____
_____
_____
_____

YEAR_____

_____
_____
_____
_____

November

14

What was your wildest dream this year?

YEAR _____
_____
_____
_____
_____

YEAR _____
_____
_____
_____
_____

YEAR _____
_____
_____
_____
_____

YEAR _____
_____
_____
_____
_____

YEAR _____
_____
_____
_____
_____

November

15

What memories do you associate with Ribbons?

YEAR_____

_____
_____
_____
_____

YEAR_____

_____
_____
_____
_____

YEAR_____

_____
_____
_____
_____

YEAR_____

_____
_____
_____
_____

YEAR_____

_____
_____
_____
_____

November

16

A good thing from today.

YEAR _____

_____
_____
_____
_____

YEAR _____

_____
_____
_____
_____

YEAR _____

_____
_____
_____
_____

YEAR _____

_____
_____
_____
_____

YEAR _____

_____
_____
_____
_____

November

17

If time or money were not a problem,
what and where do you want to study?

YEAR_____

_____
_____
_____
_____

YEAR_____

_____
_____
_____
_____

YEAR_____

_____
_____
_____
_____

YEAR_____

_____
_____
_____
_____

YEAR_____

_____
_____
_____
_____

November

18

How can I be happy and contented?

YEAR _____

_____
_____
_____
_____

YEAR _____

_____
_____
_____
_____

YEAR _____

_____
_____
_____
_____

YEAR _____

_____
_____
_____
_____

YEAR _____

_____
_____
_____
_____

19

Three favorite book characters.

YEAR_____

_____
_____
_____
_____

YEAR_____

_____
_____
_____
_____

YEAR_____

_____
_____
_____
_____

YEAR_____

_____
_____
_____
_____

YEAR_____

_____
_____
_____
_____

November

20

A moment from this month that you will always remember.

YEAR _____

_____
_____
_____
_____

YEAR _____

_____
_____
_____
_____

YEAR _____

_____
_____
_____
_____

YEAR _____

_____
_____
_____
_____

YEAR _____

_____
_____
_____
_____

November

21

Describe what happened at 5:00 PM today.

YEAR _____

_____

_____

_____

_____

YEAR _____

_____

_____

_____

_____

YEAR _____

_____

_____

_____

_____

YEAR _____

_____

_____

_____

_____

YEAR _____

_____

_____

_____

_____

November

22

When was the last time you tried something new?
What was it?

YEAR _____

_____
_____
_____
_____

YEAR _____

_____
_____
_____
_____

YEAR _____

_____
_____
_____
_____

YEAR _____

_____
_____
_____
_____

YEAR _____

_____
_____
_____
_____

November

23

What is worth celebrating?

YEAR _____

_____
_____
_____
_____

YEAR _____

_____
_____
_____
_____

YEAR _____

_____
_____
_____
_____

YEAR _____

_____
_____
_____
_____

YEAR _____

_____
_____
_____
_____

November

24

How was your work today?

YEAR _____

_____
_____
_____
_____

YEAR _____

_____
_____
_____
_____

YEAR _____

_____
_____
_____
_____

YEAR _____

_____
_____
_____
_____

YEAR _____

_____
_____
_____
_____

November

25

Do you believe in Reincarnation? Explain.

YEAR _____

_____
_____
_____
_____

YEAR _____

_____
_____
_____
_____

YEAR _____

_____
_____
_____
_____

YEAR _____

_____
_____
_____
_____

YEAR _____

_____
_____
_____
_____

November

26

Truth or Dare?

YEAR_____

_____
_____
_____
_____

YEAR_____

_____
_____
_____
_____

YEAR_____

_____
_____
_____
_____

YEAR_____

_____
_____
_____
_____

YEAR_____

_____
_____
_____
_____

November

27

Do you work better in the morning or at night?

YEAR_____

_____
_____
_____
_____

YEAR_____

_____
_____
_____
_____

YEAR_____

_____
_____
_____
_____

YEAR_____

_____
_____
_____
_____

YEAR_____

_____
_____
_____
_____

November

28

List the people you live with right now.

YEAR _____
_____
_____
_____
_____

YEAR _____
_____
_____
_____
_____

YEAR _____
_____
_____
_____
_____

YEAR _____
_____
_____
_____
_____

YEAR _____
_____
_____
_____
_____

November

29

I appreciate this day because _____.

YEAR _____

_____
_____
_____
_____

YEAR _____

_____
_____
_____
_____

YEAR _____

_____
_____
_____
_____

YEAR _____

_____
_____
_____
_____

YEAR _____

_____
_____
_____
_____

November

30

Would you rather go to the beach or climb a mountain?

YEAR _____

_____

_____

_____

_____

YEAR _____

_____

_____

_____

_____

YEAR _____

_____

_____

_____

_____

YEAR _____

_____

_____

_____

_____

YEAR _____

_____

_____

_____

_____

December

1

Favorite activity of the month and why.

YEAR _____

_____
_____
_____
_____

YEAR _____

_____
_____
_____
_____

YEAR _____

_____
_____
_____
_____

YEAR _____

_____
_____
_____
_____

YEAR _____

_____
_____
_____
_____

December

2

Mondays or Fridays?

YEAR _____

_____
_____
_____
_____

YEAR _____

_____
_____
_____
_____

YEAR _____

_____
_____
_____
_____

YEAR _____

_____
_____
_____
_____

YEAR _____

_____
_____
_____
_____

December

3

A song that made you reminisce about love.

YEAR _____

_____
_____
_____
_____

YEAR _____

_____
_____
_____
_____

YEAR _____

_____
_____
_____
_____

YEAR _____

_____
_____
_____
_____

YEAR _____

_____
_____
_____
_____

December

4

The worst thing you have ever done this year.

YEAR _____

_____
_____
_____
_____

YEAR _____

_____
_____
_____
_____

YEAR _____

_____
_____
_____
_____

YEAR _____

_____
_____
_____
_____

YEAR _____

_____
_____
_____
_____

December

5

Christmas or New Year?

YEAR _____

_____
_____
_____
_____

YEAR _____

_____
_____
_____
_____

YEAR _____

_____
_____
_____
_____

YEAR _____

_____
_____
_____
_____

YEAR _____

_____
_____
_____
_____

December

6

What is the difference between existing and living?

YEAR _____

_____
_____
_____
_____

YEAR _____

_____
_____
_____
_____

YEAR _____

_____
_____
_____
_____

YEAR _____

_____
_____
_____
_____

YEAR _____

_____
_____
_____
_____

December

7

Are you tactful?

YEAR _____

_____

_____

_____

_____

YEAR _____

_____

_____

_____

_____

YEAR _____

_____

_____

_____

_____

YEAR _____

_____

_____

_____

_____

YEAR _____

_____

_____

_____

_____

December

8

Do you believe in Karma? Explain.

YEAR _____

_____
_____
_____
_____

YEAR _____

_____
_____
_____
_____

YEAR _____

_____
_____
_____
_____

YEAR _____

_____
_____
_____
_____

YEAR _____

_____
_____
_____
_____

December

9

You best friend's most used word.

YEAR _____

_____
_____
_____
_____

YEAR _____

_____
_____
_____
_____

YEAR _____

_____
_____
_____
_____

YEAR _____

_____
_____
_____
_____

YEAR _____

_____
_____
_____
_____

December

10

Material Gifts or Memories?

YEAR _____

_____
_____
_____
_____

YEAR _____

_____
_____
_____
_____

YEAR _____

_____
_____
_____
_____

YEAR _____

_____
_____
_____
_____

YEAR _____

_____
_____
_____
_____

December

11

Last Christmas Carole you have heard.

YEAR _____

_____

_____

_____

_____

YEAR _____

_____

_____

_____

_____

YEAR _____

_____

_____

_____

_____

YEAR _____

_____

_____

_____

_____

YEAR _____

_____

_____

_____

_____

December

12

Today you should stop believing in _____.

YEAR _____

_____
_____
_____
_____

YEAR _____

_____
_____
_____
_____

YEAR _____

_____
_____
_____
_____

YEAR _____

_____
_____
_____
_____

YEAR _____

_____
_____
_____
_____

December

13

Favorite memory of this year and why.

YEAR _____

_____

_____

_____

_____

YEAR _____

_____

_____

_____

_____

YEAR _____

_____

_____

_____

_____

YEAR _____

_____

_____

_____

_____

YEAR _____

_____

_____

_____

_____

December

14

What was the best trip you ever took this year?

YEAR _____

_____
_____
_____
_____

YEAR _____

_____
_____
_____
_____

YEAR _____

_____
_____
_____
_____

YEAR _____

_____
_____
_____
_____

YEAR _____

_____
_____
_____
_____

December

15

Write a short letter to your future self.

YEAR _____

_____

_____

_____

_____

YEAR _____

_____

_____

_____

_____

YEAR _____

_____

_____

_____

_____

YEAR _____

_____

_____

_____

_____

YEAR _____

_____

_____

_____

_____

December

16

Rate from 1-10 how happy you are this year. Explain.

YEAR _____
_____
_____
_____
_____

YEAR _____
_____
_____
_____
_____

YEAR _____
_____
_____
_____
_____

YEAR _____
_____
_____
_____
_____

YEAR _____
_____
_____
_____
_____

December

17

What could you do for your family today
as a special surprise?

YEAR _____
_____
_____
_____
_____

YEAR _____
_____
_____
_____
_____

YEAR _____
_____
_____
_____
_____

YEAR _____
_____
_____
_____
_____

YEAR _____
_____
_____
_____
_____

December

18

Three new things you would like to do this Christmas.

YEAR_____
_____
_____
_____
_____

YEAR_____
_____
_____
_____
_____

YEAR_____
_____
_____
_____
_____

YEAR_____
_____
_____
_____
_____

YEAR_____
_____
_____
_____
_____

December

19

A new thing you have discovered
about yourself this year.

YEAR _____

_____
_____
_____
_____

YEAR _____

_____
_____
_____
_____

YEAR _____

_____
_____
_____
_____

YEAR _____

_____
_____
_____
_____

YEAR _____

_____
_____
_____
_____

December

20

Describe how you are feeling
about this season in one sentence.

YEAR_____
_____
_____
_____
_____

YEAR_____
_____
_____
_____
_____

YEAR_____
_____
_____
_____
_____

YEAR_____
_____
_____
_____
_____

YEAR_____
_____
_____
_____
_____

December

21

Did you live more in line with your values this year?
Explain.

YEAR _____

_____
_____
_____
_____

YEAR _____

_____
_____
_____
_____

YEAR _____

_____
_____
_____
_____

YEAR _____

_____
_____
_____
_____

YEAR _____

_____
_____
_____
_____

December

22

Describe the photos you took this month.

YEAR _____

_____
_____
_____
_____

YEAR _____

_____
_____
_____
_____

YEAR _____

_____
_____
_____
_____

YEAR _____

_____
_____
_____
_____

YEAR _____

_____
_____
_____
_____

December

23

Sweet or Salty?

YEAR _____
_____
_____
_____
_____

YEAR _____
_____
_____
_____
_____

YEAR _____
_____
_____
_____
_____

YEAR _____
_____
_____
_____
_____

YEAR _____
_____
_____
_____
_____

December

24

Is experience the best teacher? Explain.

YEAR _____

_____
_____
_____
_____

YEAR _____

_____
_____
_____
_____

YEAR _____

_____
_____
_____
_____

YEAR _____

_____
_____
_____
_____

YEAR _____

_____
_____
_____
_____

December

25

What did you have for dinner on Christmas Eve?

YEAR _____

_____
_____
_____
_____

YEAR _____

_____
_____
_____
_____

YEAR _____

_____
_____
_____
_____

YEAR _____

_____
_____
_____
_____

YEAR _____

_____
_____
_____
_____

December

Who did you spend your Christmas with?

YEAR _____
_____
_____
_____
_____

YEAR _____
_____
_____
_____
_____

YEAR _____
_____
_____
_____
_____

YEAR _____
_____
_____
_____
_____

YEAR _____
_____
_____
_____
_____

December

Describe your Christmas outfit.

YEAR _____

_____

_____

_____

_____

YEAR _____

_____

_____

_____

_____

YEAR _____

_____

_____

_____

_____

YEAR _____

_____

_____

_____

_____

YEAR _____

_____

_____

_____

_____

December

28

What was the best present
you have received this Christmas?

YEAR _____
_____
_____
_____
_____

YEAR _____
_____
_____
_____
_____

YEAR _____
_____
_____
_____
_____

YEAR _____
_____
_____
_____
_____

YEAR _____
_____
_____
_____
_____

December

29

How would you describe your mood today?

YEAR _____

_____
_____
_____
_____

YEAR _____

_____
_____
_____
_____

YEAR _____

_____
_____
_____
_____

YEAR _____

_____
_____
_____
_____

YEAR _____

_____
_____
_____
_____

December

30

Have you met your goals for this year? Explain.

YEAR _____
_____
_____
_____
_____

YEAR _____
_____
_____
_____
_____

YEAR _____
_____
_____
_____
_____

YEAR _____
_____
_____
_____
_____

YEAR _____
_____
_____
_____
_____

December

31

One word that best describes your year.

YEAR_____

_____
_____
_____
_____

YEAR_____

_____
_____
_____
_____

YEAR_____

_____
_____
_____
_____

YEAR_____

_____
_____
_____
_____

YEAR_____

_____
_____
_____
_____

YOU MAY LOVE IT

CONCLUSION

Thank you again for buying this book! I hope you enjoyed with my book. Finally, if you like this book, please take the time to share your thoughts and post a review on Amazon. It'd be greatly appreciated! Thank you!

Next Steps
– Write me an honest review about the book –
I truly value your opinion and thoughts and I will incorporate them into my next book, which is already underway.

Made in the USA
Monee, IL
09 June 2021